Regina Public Library
BOOK SALE ITEM
Non-returnable

freestyle

SKATEBOARDING TRICKS

flat ground rails transitions

D0047940

Acknowledgments

A huge thank you to all the skaters who gave up their time to help me write this book: Sophie, Matt, Zane, Raoul, Quayde, Kaitlyn, Luke, Dylan and Phil. Your love of the sport shone through for all to see and the book would not have been possible without this dedication.

Another massive thank you must go to April Ward (www.aprilwardphotography.com) who has captured the energy and freedom of the sport in her magnificent photographs throughout the book. Terrific job.

Sean D'Arcy

Thanks to my mum and dad, sisters Jasmine and Zoe, Element, Adidas and Beyond Skate, Jarvis, Quayde, Luke, Dylan, Sophie, Matt, Raul, Kaitlyn, Matt R, Mitch B, Mitchy C, Bag, Benmneb, Maciek, Robbie, James, Brodie, Tyson, Joel, Lang, Skateboarding, South Park, the City of Perth and the rest of my family, interests and friends. Peace!

Phillip Marshall

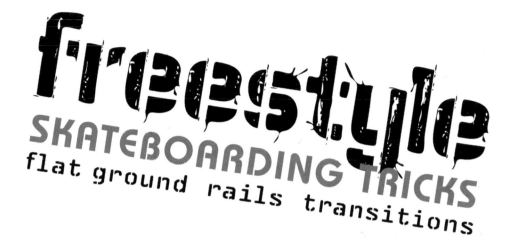

freestyle
SKATEBOARDING TRICKS
flat ground rails transitions

SEAN D'ARCY AND
PHILLIP MARSHALL

A FIREFLY BOOK

Published by Firefly Books Ltd. 2010

Copyright © 2010 Sean D'Arcy and Phillip Marshall

All rights reserved. No part of this publication may be reproduced, stored in a retrieval system, or transmitted in any form or by any means, electronic, mechanical, photocopying, recording or otherwise, without the prior written permission of the Publisher.

First printing

Publisher Cataloging-in-Publication Data (U.S.)

D'Arcy, Sean.
    Freestyle skateboarding tricks : flat ground, rails and transitions / Sean D'Arcy.
[128] p. : col. photos. ; cm.
ISBN-13: 978-1-55407-666-6 (pbk.)
ISBN-10: 1-55407-666-8
1. Skateboarding — Juvenile literature. I. Title.
796.2/1 dc22   GV859.8D37 2010

**Library and Archives Canada
Cataloguing in Publication**

D'Arcy, Sean
    Freestyle skateboarding tricks : flat ground, rails and transitions / Sean D'Arcy.
ISBN-13: 978-1-55407-666-6
ISBN-10: 1-55407-666-8
    1. Skateboarding — Juvenile literature. I. Title.
GV859.8.D36 2010   j796.22   C2010-900125-7

Published in the United States by
Firefly Books (U.S.) Inc.
P.O. Box 1338, Ellicott Station
Buffalo, New York 14205

Published in Canada by
Firefly Books Ltd.
66 Leek Crescent
Richmond Hill, Ontario L4B 1H1

Printed in China

Freestyle Skateboarding was developed by
A&C Black Publishers Ltd
36 Soho Square, London, W1D 3QY

Cover design by James Watson
Text design and typesetting by James Watson
Cover photograph © shutterstock.com
Inside photographs © April Ward

Note: It is always the responsibility of the individual to assess his or her own fitness capability before participating in any training activity. Whilst every effort has been made to ensure the content of this book is as technically accurate as possible, neither the author nor the publishers can accept responsibility for any injury or loss sustained as a result of the use of this material.

CONTENTS

Introduction

Introduction

Many people are amazed to discover that skateboarding is over 50 years old. In the 1950s surfers in California got the idea to try to surf the streets when there were no waves to ride. Skateboarding has gone through some huge surges in popularity since then, the first in the early 1960s, then again in the mid-70s and mid-80s, but now it has established itself as a genuine sport. Skateboarding is now being considered for inclusion in the Olympics.

Freestyle Skateboarding Tricks has moves that have developed throughout the history of the sport — such as the Boneless, which is one of the earliest tricks — all the way to the modern flip tricks of today.

This book is divided into three chapters: Flat Ground; Rails, Slides & Grinds; and Grabs & Transitions. Flat Ground is when it is just you, the board and the ground. The only limits are in your mind. The Rails chapter is all about balance and style. The last chapter, Grabs & Transitions, is when the tricks get bigger and higher.

Enough reading about skateboarding and time to start doing some magic with that board, so read on.

01

Flat Ground

Flat Ground is when it is just you, the board and the ground. The only limits are in your mind.

THE OLLIE

The Ollie is the way you get your board to fly. This is something you need to learn for many of the tricks later on in this book.

Foot Position

Front foot over the front bolts, back foot on the middle of the tail of the board.

Step 1

Crouch down.

Step 2

Take your weight off your front foot and slam the tail down hard with your back foot.

Common Problem

My board always goes off to the side when I pop it.

Make sure your back foot is in the middle of the tail when you do Step 2.

Step 3

Then hop off your back foot and ride the board as it pops up into the air.

Remix

A fantastic remix is to "bone" the Ollie. When the board is in the air stay crouched down and push the board forward with your front foot.

Secret

At first do an Ollie with the board still, and hold on to something, like a fence, for balance, so you can get your action right.

Phil's Tip ‹‹

Don't worry about how high you go when first learning an Ollie. Just focus on getting Steps 2 and 3 right.

NOLLIE

A Nollie is basically the opposite of an Ollie. Hence the name Nose Ollie or Nollie.

Foot Position

Toes of your front foot in the middle of the nose, back foot in front of the back bolts.

Step 1

Crouch down.

Step 2

Take your weight off your back foot and slam the nose down hard with your front foot.

Common Problem

I never get enough height to level out.

Make sure you are taking the weight off your back foot in Step 2, as you could be holding the board down.

Step 3

Hop off your front foot and slide your back foot up the board to level out in the air, and then land on all four wheels.

Remix

Mastering the Nollie is invaluable, as later on in the book you need to be able to do one to get out of some of the tricks.

Secret

Bend your knees to cushion the landing in Step 3.

Phil's Tip ‹‹

Just work on popping the board up to begin with, and worry about leveling the board out later.

KICKFLIP

The day Phil first landed a KickFlip he was so excited he called up his best friend to tell him, and found out his friend had just landed his first one too!

Foot Position

Front foot pointing forward slightly, just under the front bolts, back foot on the middle of the tail.

Step 1

Crouch down, take your weight off your front foot and slam the tail down hard with your back foot.

Step 2

Hop off your back foot, then slide your front foot up the board and flick through the near side of the nose of the board with your toes.

Phil's Tip ◄◄

Phil learned the KickFlip on grass holding on to a fence. It meant he could jump up higher and practice his landings easier.

Step 3

The board rotates sideways 360 degrees toward you. Wait for the board to level out and land on the bolts.

Remix

A wonderful remix for the KickFlip is to do it going backward. It uses exactly the same steps, but has a whole different feel of its own when done fakey (backward).

Secret

Keep your weight forward so when you land you don't pop the board up again.

Common Problem

My board always lands primo (on its side).

If the wheels are facing away from you when the board lands, then you are flicking too hard in Step 2 and getting too much rotation. If the wheels are facing you then you need to flick harder.

HEELFLIP

You could say the HeelFlip is the complete opposite of the KickFlip — it gives you just as good a feeling when you land it.

Foot Position

Front foot straight on the board, with your heel just under the front bolts and your toes hanging over the edge, back foot on the middle of the tail.

Step 1

Crouch down and take your weight off your front foot and slam the tail down hard with your back foot.

Step 2

Hop off your back foot, then slide your front foot up the board and flick through the far side of the nose of the board with your heel.

Phil's Tip «

In Step 2 just flick with your foot. Don't throw your leg forward or you will overbalance and land in front of your board.

Step 3

The board will rotate sideways 360 degrees away from you. Wait for the board to level out, and land on the bolts.

Remix

A really cool remix is to throw in a 180 with this trick. So read on to learn the next trick and then combine the two together.

Secret

Be careful and focus. It is very easy to kick the board away from you in Step 2.

Common Problem

The board always lands away from me.

You are putting too much pressure on the board with your front foot and then kicking it away. Relax and remember to slide your front foot up the board, then flick the nose.

FRONTSIDE 180

When some skaters first learn to Ollie they can drag the board sideways. If that was you then you were born to do the Frontside 180.

Foot Position

Front foot over the front bolts, back foot on the middle of the tail.

Step 1

Crouch down, then swing your left arm out behind you to twist your upper body around.

Step 2

Take your weight off your front foot and slam the tail down hard with your back foot.

Phil's Tip «

Everything to get you through the 180 is in the shoulders, so really wind up and twist that upper body.

Step 3

Next, hop off your back foot and slide your front foot up to the nose. Guide the board around 180 degrees as it pops up into the air.

Remix

A great remix is to swing your upper body around the other way in Step 1 to make it a Backside 180. Looks awesome and you can get in two tricks for the price of one as everything else is the same.

Secret

When learning this one it is tough to make the full 180, but you can build up to it gradually.

Common Problem

I never make it all the way through 180.

Two things: either you need to Ollie higher to give yourself more time in the air, or you need to swing those shoulders around more.

FRONTSIDE 360

This is a great trick to do over any hips (the edge where two slopes meet) in your skate park. It looks great and the hip gives you plenty of air time to complete it.

Foot Position

Front foot over the front bolts with your toes hanging slightly over the edge, back foot on the near side of the tail.

Step 1

Bend your knees, crouch down, then swing your arm out behind you to twist your upper body around.

Phil's Tip

In Step 1, to get the full 360 it may help to cross your arm in front of your body before you swing it behind, for more rotation.

Step 2

Take your weight off your front foot and slam the tail down and forward with your back foot.

Step 3

Hop off your back foot and slide your front foot across the board up to the nose and guide the board around 360 degrees as it pops up into the air.

Remix

A fabulous remix is a Backside 360. Some skaters (including Phil) find it easier to do a Backside 360 than a Frontside.

Secret

Don't try a 360 until you can regularly over-rotate a 180. Just gradually build up to a 360 by rotating 180 degrees and reverting (pivoting on the back wheel) the rest of the way.

Common Problem

I always lose my balance and fall backward.

You are not just twisting your upper body in Step 1, but actually throwing yourself backward. Remember, you must keep your weight over the board.

POWER SLIDE

Basically this is how to drift on a skateboard. Not only does this trick look great, it just makes the most fantastic noise.

Foot Position

Front foot over the front bolts, back foot on the middle of the tail.

Step 1

Skating forward, quickly shift all your weight to your front foot.

Phil's Tip

You can use the Power Slide to act as a brake if you are skating downhill.

Step 2

Using your back foot, push the tail 90 degrees so the board slides forward and sideways.

Step 3

Drag the tail back 90 degrees.

Remix

This is really a bit of a cheat but it still looks good. If you push out too hard in Step 2 and go over 90 degrees, then just do the slide and revert through 180 degrees. You still get the noise and the slide, and you still look good.

Secret

You need hard wheels to do this. If your wheels are too soft they will grip, not slide.

Common Problem
I can just never get the board to slide.

You need to go faster as the Power Slide can act as a brake. It is worth it so you can hear that wonderful drifting noise.

SHUV-IT

This is a neat trick simply because the board moves so quickly.

Foot Position

Front foot pointing slightly forward just under the front bolts, sole of your back foot on the far rim of the tail.

Step 1

Crouch down.

Step 2

Jump off with both feet, but with your back foot shove the tail of the board behind you.

Phil's Tip «

You don't need to jump up really high, just get yourself off the board.

Step 3

The board will slide 180 degrees. Wait for it to come all the way around and catch it with your front foot, then land.

Remix

A superb remix for this is to Pop Shuv-it. Change the position of your back foot so it's in the middle of the tail, and push down and shove the board backward in Step 2. The board now pops up as it rotates 180 degrees, adding a whole extra dimension to the trick.

Secret

When the board rotates through 180 degrees it will finish slightly in front of where it was before, so in Step 2 jump forward otherwise you will miss the board.

Common Problem

The board always lands primo.

You are pushing down as well as shoving the board in Step 2, so you are making the board flip.

VERIAL KICKFLIP

The Verial KickFlip has got a reputation for being a surfer's trick as most surfers seem to find it easy to land the board. No one knows why.

Foot Position

Front foot pointing forward slightly just under the front bolts, sole of your back foot on the far rim of the tail.

Step 1

Crouch down and take your weight off your front foot, slam the tail down hard and shove it toward you with your back foot.

Step 2

Hop off your back foot then slide your front foot up the board and flick through the near side of the nose of the board with your toes.

Common Problem

I always land primo and I can't seem to stop doing it.

Check whether you're flicking through the nose of the board or through the side. If the wheels land facing you then you could be going through the side.

35

Step 3

The board will flip 360 degrees as well as rotate 180 degrees. Be patient and wait for the board to level out before you land on the bolts with your weight forward.

Remix

An unbelievable remix is to do a Big Spin which is where you do everything the same, but when you hop you spin your body around and land facing the other way. Not easy — this requires lots of practice — but it's worth every hour.

Secret

Remember the board is rotating as you go through Step 2, so your front foot will need to go straight up the board to flick through the near side of the nose.

Phil's Tip ◄◄

Get your Pop Shuv-its locked before trying this.

CRAB WALK

This is one of the fun things Phil learned to do when he was first starting out. You could say it looks a bit like Frankenstein's monster walking on a skateboard.

Foot Position

Stand on the board with your feet apart with each foot past the bolts at either end.

Step 1

Put all your weight on your left foot and using your upper body twist the right end of the board forward a bit.

Step 2

Now put all your weight on your right foot and twist the left end of the board forward.

Phil's Tip

Don't do this if you want to impress anyone watching you.

Common Problem

I always fall forward off the board.

Remember, you need to have your weight over the board. It sounds like you are leaning forward and overbalancing.

Step 3

Keep repeating Steps 1 and 2 and you are Crab Walking.

Remix

A great remix is to Revert Crab Walk, which means you keep pivoting 180 degrees on your board to walk forward.

Secret

Don't walk too slow or the board will slide from side to side and make it difficult to balance.

HARDFLIP

This is the right name for this trick. It is hard to do, but that means less people can do it, so stick with it and you will be one of the few who can.

Foot Position

Front foot just below the front bolts pointing out at 45 degrees, back foot on the near-side of the tail.

Step 1

Crouch down, take your weight off your front foot and slam the tail down hard, shoving it away from you with your back foot.

Step 2

Jump up as high as you can off your back foot, then slide your front foot up the board diagonally and flick the board with your toes.

Common Problem

The board always hits my legs.

You have to get your front foot out of the way to let the board go through your legs. Make that jump in Step 2 as high as you can.

Step 3

The board will flip and go end over end between your legs. Wait for it to level out and then land on the bolts.

Remix

A HardFlip is difficult enough, but a really tricky remix is to do a Nollie HardFlip. Basically you pop the nose and flick out the tail. Boy, does it look good though.

Secret

The HardFlip is all about getting the board high enough when you pop in Step 1, so you really need to be able to get some good height before attempting Steps 2 and 3.

Phil's Tip ««

It is best to practice the HardFlip holding on to a fence, as the board coming down at the wrong time can bring tears to your eyes.

TREFLIP (OR 360 FLIP)

Λ friend of Phil's does amazing TreFlips. If he sees someone do it with a different style he will practice until he can copy them. No matter how it's done the TreFlip always gets a good reaction from a crowd.

Foot Position

Front foot just below the front bolts pointing out at 45 degrees, back foot on the far side of the tail.

Step 1

Crouch down and hop up high off your back foot as you scoop the tail down hard and in toward you.

43

Step 2

Slide your front foot up the board and flick through the near-side of the nose of the board with your toes.

Phil's Tip

After you have flicked in Step 2 you really need to spread your legs in the air otherwise the board will hit you as it rotates through 360 degrees.

Step 3

The board will rotate through 360 degrees while flipping. Wait for the board to level out, and land on the bolts with your weight on your front foot.

Remix

This insane remix is a Bigger Flip. You do the TreFlip as normal, but when you catch the board in Step 3 you spin 180 degrees and land the other way around. Incredible when you see it done in front of you.

Secret

You need to get the Pop Shuv-it 360 locked before trying the TreFlip.

Common Problem

My board always lands wheels up.

This is a huge back-foot trick. Your back foot does all the work and you are not popping the board hard enough to give it enough height to rotate fully.

TICTAC

TicTacing is how you build up speed on flat ground without taking your foot off the board, and it's a fun way to develop good balance.

Foot Position

Front foot over the front bolts, back foot on the center of the tail.

Step 1

Put your weight on your back foot just enough to lift the front wheels off the ground.

Step 2

Push the nose of the board to the left with your front foot and land on the front wheels.

Common Problem

It always takes me forever to get up any speed.

You need to drop the front of the board down a bit as it sounds like you are going higher than you need to.

Step 3

Lift the front wheels again and this time push the nose over to the right with your front foot. Keep repeating Steps 1 to 3 until you have picked up enough speed.

Remix

When Phil was younger he used to have TicTac races with his friends. By the way, he has never said whether he used to win the races.

Secret

You don't need to swing all the way left, then all the way right. Just do quick little swings from left to right and the speed will build up fast.

Phil's Tip ‹‹

You don't need to lift the front wheels high for this to work.

MANUAL

Just about everyone who has ever stepped on a board has tried to balance on the back wheels. This is how to do it.

Foot Position

Front foot just on the front bolts, back foot on the center of the tail.

Step 1

Lift your weight off your front foot and on to your back foot.

49

Step 2

Allow the nose to come up, but use your front foot to push it down gently until the board is balanced on the back wheels.

Common Problem
I always scrape the tail.

You have to use both feet for a Manual, so push down more with your front foot in Step 2 to lift the tail off the ground.

Step 3

Roll forward with your arms out to help you balance, then push down with your front foot to land the front wheels.

Remix

A wonderful remix which gets a good reaction from a crowd is to Manual on the front wheels. It is harder, but if you can get your balance for a Manual then you can try a Nose Manual — it is well worth it.

Secret

Make sure your weight is through the sole of your back foot otherwise your heel might hit the ground in Step 3.

Phil's Tip <<

Try to find out what height you balance at by practicing on grass as this way the wheels won't suddenly slide from under you.

IMPOSSIBLE

The only easy thing about this trick is it is easy to see how it got its name. Worth every day of practice it takes to lock in, your mission, should you choose to accept it, is to do the Impossible.

Foot Position

Position your front foot anywhere on the board so you can get it out of the way when the Impossible starts. Your back foot should be in the center of the tail.

Step 1

Crouch down, take your weight off your front foot and slam the tail down hard with your back foot and hop up high.

Step 2

Get your front foot out of the way and as the board pops up, scoop the tail forward with your back foot. The board wraps vertically around your back foot.

Phil's Tip ◄◄

The best way to learn an Impossible is to practice the scooping motion in Step 2 on its own. Just hop your front foot on the ground — this way you get a feel for the movement needed.

Step 3

When the board has done the vertical 360 degrees your back foot is still on the board, so now put your front foot down and the Impossible just became possible.

Remix

An impossible remix for the Impossible is a Front Foot Impossible. Phil has only ever seen it done twice and he says it is simply amazing.

Secret

With an Impossible, your back foot can end up past the back bolts toward the middle of the board, so in Step 3 place your front foot as far up the board as you can to help with balance.

Common Problem
Mine never looks right.

If it looks more like a Shuv-it 360 then remember to scoop forward in Step 2. You are pushing it sideways too and so the board doesn't go vertical.

NO-COMPLY

A fabulous trick. The first time you see this it looks like the skater fell off, then somehow managed to get back on the board. A top skater makes this look so smooth.

Foot Position

Front foot can be anywhere you feel comfortable as this is a back-foot trick, back foot on the center of the tail.

Step 1

Step off the board with your front foot.

Step 2

Push down on the tail with your back foot to pop the board up into the air.

Phil's Tip <<

Don't pop too hard when first trying this. Just get the motion of getting back on the board locked first.

Step 3

Jump off your front foot and back on to the board to land it and roll away.

Remix

A cool remix is to pop quite low, scoop the board and do a No-Comply 180. I can guarantee that someone in the crowd will think you have messed up and won't be able to figure out how you got back on so quickly.

Secret

In Step 2 try to push forward with your back foot as well to maintain some contact with the board.

Common Problem

I never seem to be able to land on the board.

You really have to watch the board and commit to it. It is all about the feel so practice with the pop really low and work up to doing it higher.

BONELESS

A retro move from the 70s before skaters discovered the Ollie, this was the way that you got the board up and over stuff.

Foot Position

Front foot and back foot wherever you feel comfortable.

Step 1

Step your front foot off the board.

Step 2

Lift the board up with your hand while keeping your back foot on the board.

Step 3

Jump up off your front foot and sail through the air before landing on the board and rolling away.

Remix

This one takes it to the next level. Use your back hand to grab the back side of the board through your legs in the starting position, then twist the board when you jump in Step 3.

Secret

Use your hand to level the board out in Step 3.

Phil's Tip ‹‹

Just focus on lifting the board up with your hand at the start, as it feels funny not to Ollie the board.

Rails, Slides & Grinds

Rail tricks are all about balance and style. You have to know how to Ollie to do the tricks in this chapter.

BACKSIDE BOARDSLIDE

The classic rail trick, the backslide boardslide is a bit of a board-snapper. Every skater has their own story of when the board snapped on them.

Step 1

Approach the rail and be almost parallel to it when you Ollie.

Step 2

Use your front foot to guide the nose of the board over the rail, land the middle of the board at 90 degrees to the rail, and slide.

Phil's Tip ◄◄

Turn your shoulders in Step 2 to help guide the board on to the rail.

Common Problem

The board always shoots away in front of me in Step 2.

Simple: when you land in Step 2 you are leaning back and so overbalance.

Step 3

As you approach the end, twist your shoulders and guide the nose of the board back straight so you can roll away.

Remix

A fantastic remix is to LipSlide — approach the rail from the opposite side, and in Step 2 guide the tail of the board over the rail. This can feel really uncomfortable to some skaters at first, but it looks amazing.

Secret

When learning this one, just Ollie on and put one foot on the board to slide it along, with the other foot on the ground, until you get the motion locked.

FRONTSIDE 50-50

Phil has been doing 50-50s for a while now and lately he has been trying them on really high stuff. But he had lots of practice on low rails first.

Step 1

Approach the rail and be almost parallel to it when you Ollie.

Step 2

Land on the rail so you grind along on both the front and back trucks.

Phil's Tip ‹‹

Point your front shoulder the way you want to go and this will help with your balance.

Step 3

As you approach the end of the rail, push down on the tail to pop the nose up and roll away smiling.

Remix

A sweet remix. Halfway along the 50-50 grind just pop the nose up and Manual to the end of the rail. Or you could turn a 50-50 into a 5-0 (see next page).

Secret

It makes landing easier if you land back trucks first and then front trucks.

Common Problem
I cannot stay on the board as it grinds.

If you fall over the rail then your Ollie is too big, if you fall away from the rail then you are too far away when you Ollie.

5-0

Phil's favorite way to do the 5-0 used to be Backside, but now he prefers Frontside. He has no idea why.

Step 1

Approach the rail and be almost parallel to it when you Ollie.

Phil's Tip ◄◄

Learn how to do a 50-50 before you try a 5-0.

Step 2

Land on the rail on your back trucks, then keep your weight on your back foot and Manual as you grind.

Common Problem

I never lock straight on the rail and always slip over the rail.

Check the angle you are approaching at — it sounds like it is too big.

Step 3

Use your front foot to keep the board straight. To make a clean exit just push your back foot down more as you slide off the rail and roll away.

Remix

There are two amazing remixes for this one: the Suski and the Salad. In Step 3, instead of keeping the board straight with the rail use your front foot to point the nose of the board out 45 degrees to the side. A Suski points the board behind your back foot and a Salad points the nose in front.

Secret

The approach is extremely important, as the more you twist into a 5-0 the harder it is to land.

NOSE GRIND

A Nose Grind always gets a good reaction from a crowd. People just seem to love it. You could call this the opposite of a 5-0.

Step 1

Approach the rail and be almost parallel to it when you Ollie. This time start with your front foot closer to the nose of the board.

Step 2

When airborne, push your nose down with your front foot, so you land on the rail with your front trucks. Keep your back wheels up and grind the rail.

Phil's Tip ◀◀

A great way to practice is to Ollie on to a box and Nose Manual. It is exactly the same action and you don't need to worry about balancing on the rail.

Common Problem

I never get to the end of the rail.

Sounds like you are pushing the nose right down onto the rail, so it is acting like a brake. Remember: only the front trucks on the rail.

Step 3

As you approach the end do a Nollie to lift the board up, then land it and roll away.

Remix

You need lots of speed and a long rail, but you could go from a Nose Grind to a 50-50 in the one run. Looks sick.

Secret

When you have perfected a 50-50, practice doing a Nollie off the rail, so that when you learn a Nose Grind it is easier to get off the rail.

CROOKED GRIND

A Crooked Grind looks totally wrong at the beginning, but when the crowd sees you stay balanced and grind, it ends up looking totally right.

Step 1

Approach the rail at a 45 degree angle and do your Ollie with your front foot closer to the nose of the board.

Step 2

When airborne, push your nose down with your front foot so you land on the rail with one front wheel on the rail and one off. Grind along on your front truck, one wheel and the nose of the board.

Phil's Tip <<

Work on just stalling on the rail first so you can get the height and angle of your Ollie right.

Common Problem

I never get the wheel on and end up doing a Nose Slide.

You just need to get your Ollies that little bit higher.

Step 3

As you approach the end, do a Nollie and turn your shoulders to guide the board straight, then roll away smiling.

Remix

An unbelievable remix is to OverCrook when you Ollie over the rail, then twist your nose around and grind in exactly the same way, but this time you grind on the opposite side of the rail to your approach. Just looks like it shouldn't happen.

Secret

When first learning, don't try to grind along the length of the rail, just do the last bit. As you get better go farther and farther back down the rail.

BACKSIDE TAILSLIDE

Phil prefers to do this trick Backside. Although this is harder for most skaters Phil finds it easier than Frontside.

Step 1

Approach the rail at a 45 degree angle and do your Ollie with your front foot below the front bolts.

Step 2

Twist your front shoulder and guide the nose away from the rail with your front foot. Land just the tail on the rail with your back truck jammed against it.

Common Problem

I always seem to slide off the rail and cannot get the grind.

Your approach is too parallel, so when you do the Backside 180 you keep rotating and your tail just slides across the rail instead of locking against it. Remember: approach at a 45 degree angle.

Step 3

Grind along with your weight on your back foot. Twist your front shoulder in the direction you are going to guide the nose forward, and roll away.

Remix

A smooth remix, because it suits the flow of the trick, is to come off the rail fakey (backward). As Phil says, it just seems to be the natural way to finish it.

Secret

Make sure you approach the rail at a 45 degree angle so that the back truck really hits the rail.

Phil's Tip «

As you grind, look over your shoulder so you can see where you are going.

FRONTSIDE SMITH GRIND

If you lock a Smith Grind right you can grind forever, so it is a good trick to know for when you find that long, straight rail you have been dreaming about.

Step 1

Approach the rail at a 45 degree angle and do your Ollie with your front foot just below the front bolts.

Step 2

Twist your front shoulder and guide the nose away from the rail with your front foot. Land the back truck on the rail with your nose pointing downward.

Phil's Tip

It helps to get your 50-50s locked before you try the Smith Grind.

Step 3

Keep all your weight on your back foot as you grind, then push down on the tail and pop off the end of the rail.

Remix

A superb remix of a Smith Grind is the Feeble Grind. This is the same, with the back trucks on the rail and nose pointing down, but you jump over the rail before you grind. It looks impossible but you can do it now.

Secret

This is totally a back-foot trick and your front foot is just there to guide the nose.

Common Problem

I always go over during the grind and my board seems to stick.

You are leaning too far forward. Remember all the weight should be on your back foot — you have some weight on your front foot which is why you fall forward.

NOSE SLIDE

A Nose Slide is smooth, looks good and just makes you feel like you are doing what you were born to do when you nail it.

Step 1

Approach the rail at a 45 degree angle and do your Ollie.

Step 2

Land the nose of the board on the rail so that your board sticks out a 90 degree angle to the rail.

Phil's Tip «

You can practice balancing on the nose of the board on curbs without even doing an Ollie.

Common Problem

I always bail on the landing.

Don't forget the Nollie, and to turn your shoulders in Step 3, and you will land it.

Step 3

Keep your weight down on your front foot and slide. Push down on the nose to Nollie, turn your shoulders at the end of the rail and roll away.

Remix

This one is for the really advanced skaters. As you are Nose Sliding, do a Nollie and switch to a Crooked Grind. It looks as good as it sounds.

Secret

You must keep your weight on your front foot or the tail end will drop and you will lose the Nose Slide.

FRONTSIDE BLUNTSLIDE

This is without a doubt one of the most amazing tricks there is. Everybody watches when you are dropping tricks of this standard.

Step 1

Approach the rail and be almost parallel to it when you Ollie. You really need to rocket the Ollie so the front wheels go really high.

Step 2

Keep your shoulders straight with the rail, but use your front foot to guide the nose above the rail. Land the back of the back wheels on the rail and slide.

Phil's Tip ◄◄

You have to keep your shoulders straight with the rail. Only use your legs to guide the board.

Step 3

Keep your weight on your back foot as you approach the end of the rail, guide the nose with your front foot forward and roll away.

Remix

A super hard remix where you really need your BluntSlide locked, is to KickFlip into it. Super hard but looks super good.

Secret

Make sure your back toes stay on the board, and don't hang over the edge of the tail and catch on the rail.

Common Problem
I can never land a Frontside BluntSlide.

You are not guiding the nose forward, so you are landing sideways and falling, which is simply the law of gravity.

FRONTSIDE NOSE BLUNTSLIDE

A BluntSlide is amazing, but I don't think they have invented the words yet to properly describe a Nose BluntSlide.

Step 1

Approach the rail and be almost parallel to it when you Ollie. Slide your front foot up the board to the nose.

Phil's Tip ◀◀

Practice doing Nose BluntSlides on flat surfaces first so you don't have to worry about falling off the rail. Once you have the motion locked then try to land it on a rail.

Step 2

Twist your upper body and use your front foot to guide the board around 90 degrees. Push down with your front foot to land the nose over the rail and slide on your front wheels.

Step 3

Push down on the nose to Nollie and use your back foot to guide the board straight and roll away.

Remix

An outstanding remix is to go for a Backside Nose Bluntside. It has a completely different feel to it from Frontside, but looks just as good.

Secret

It helps to think of this as just a nose slide with your front wheels getting in the way of a flat slide. Don't think about overshooting the rail. You can do it.

Common Problem

My back wheels always clip the rail when I get off.

Two things: either Nollie harder to push away from the rail, or don't forget to use your back foot to guide the board straight and away from the rails.

WILLY GRIND

This is also called the Booger Grind. Stunning trick, but not too sure I want to find out any more than necessary about those names.

Step 1

Approach the rail and be almost parallel to it when you Ollie.

Step 2

Land the front trucks on the rail with your tail pointing down below the rail. Keep your weight over the front bolts and grind.

Phil's Tip <<

Willy Grinds are perfect to do on high rails.

Step 3

As you come off the rail push down hard with your front foot and roll away.

Remix

A fabulous remix is to go from a Willy Grind to 50-50. You just have to push down on the nose to bring the tail up and guide it on to the rails. It shows you have total control over the board.

Secret

Keep your weight on your front bolts as you grind, but don't push down otherwise you will bring the tail up.

Common Problem

I can never land a Willy Grind. The tail is always up and when I push it down I fall.

You are simply doing too high an Ollie. Just gently pop the nose up and lock it on. You don't need a big Ollie.

03

Transitions

This is when the fun starts as now the tricks start getting bigger and higher.

GRABS

Grabs are fun. This is when you get as much air as possible, then grab the board in different ways and hold it for as long as you can while you are up there.

Indy

Grab the front side of the board with your back hand. Nice one.

Nose Grab

Grab the nose with your front hand.

Tail Grab

Grab the tail with your back hand.

Melon

Grab the back side of the board with
your front hand.

TuckKnee

Your back hand grabs the front side of
the board and your back knee touches
the board as well. Awesome.

Stalefish

Your back hand grabs the back of the board behind your legs.

CannonBall

Grab the nose with your front hand and
the tail with your back hand. Smile for
the camera.

RocketAir

Have both of your feet on the tail and
both hands on the nose. Nice one.

AirWalk

Catch the nose of the board with your front hand and walk on air next to the board.

Mute

Your front hand grabs the front side of the board.

Crail

Your back hand grabs the nose of the board.

Roast Beef

Reach your hand between your legs and grab the back side of the board. Tricky.

DROP-IN

When Phil was teaching a friend of his to Drop-In he told him to make sure he slammed the nose down. His friend did as he was told, but a little too hard and face planted, knocking his two front teeth out. Please don't let that happen to you.

Foot Position

Stand on the tail with your back foot and hold the board in place on the edge. Place your front foot on the front bolts.

Step 1

Keep your shoulders straight, eyes on where you are going to land and begin to lean over the edge.

Step 2

Slam the nose down with your front foot and roll away.

Remix

A smooth remix for this is to skate into it. Skate along, but as you come to the edge just do a Manual over it, then Drop-In.

Secret

Gradually build up by starting to Drop-In on banks or mini ramps, so you can get your confidence up before you try the bigger drops.

Phil's Tip «

You can practice this when you are on flat ground. Just stand on the tail and get used to the motion of slamming the nose down.

ROCK 2 FAKEY

Go to any skate park in any part of the world and within minutes you will see someone Rock 2 Fakey. You just have to know how to do it.

Foot Position

Your front foot over the front bolts, back foot on the middle of the tail of the board.

Step 1

As you approach the coping on the quarter pipe, push down with your back foot to lift the front wheels up.

Step 2

Shift your weight to your front foot and push the wheels down over the coping.

Phil's Tip ‹‹

When learning this one just drop the front wheels over the coping — don't try to go too far over at this stage.

Step 3

Shift your weight back to your back foot and lift the front wheels up clear off the coping and roll away backward.

Remix

Rock N Roll is a wonderful remix to this one. Instead of going back Fakey, in Step 3 pivot 180 degrees on your back wheels and roll down forward. It just looks really cool.

Secret

Remember to lift the front wheels up in Step 3, because otherwise they will hang up on the coping and you will be rolling down the slope without a board.

Common Problem

I lose the board on the Fakey every time.

You are not lifting the front wheels up in Step 3. Try standing more on the tail of the board.

BACKSIDE DISASTER

Great name for a great trick. Not sure where the name came from, but I can imagine it has something to do with the number of times you fall over learning this one.

Foot Position

Front foot pointing forward just under the front bolts with the sole of your back foot on the far rim of the tail.

Step 1

As you approach the coping, twist your upper body across in front of you and use your back foot to scoop the tail around.

Step 2

Lock the middle of the board on the coping, with you now facing back down the slope.

Phil's Tip ◄◄

Practice your back reverts before you attempt a Backside Disaster.

Step 3

Lean forward and slide your front foot up and push down on the nose to lift the tail up and over the coping and roll down.

Remix

A wicked remix is to go higher, and to Ollie into the Disaster and slam down the board in Step 2. Gives the trick some grunt.

Secret

Timing is essential — you need to get your pace up to give you time to twist at the top.

Common Problem

I always overbalance at the top and never make it back down.

Remember — you have to keep your weight over the board. It sounds like you are throwing yourself around and not just twisting.

AXLE STALL

One of Phil's friends started saluting when they Axle Stalled the board. It has stuck and now he salutes all the time.

Foot Position

Front foot over the front bolts, back foot on the middle of the tail of the board.

Step 1

Approach at a slight angle and let the front wheels go above the coping.

Step 2

Using your front foot guide the nose around 90 degrees while allowing the back trucks to rest on top of the coping, then land the front trucks on the coping too.

Phil's Tip ❮❮

Practice how to get out of Axle Stall in Step 3 first before you try the trick.

Step 3

Use your back foot to push down on the tail to lift the nose up. Guide it with your front foot through another 90 degrees to slam down on the slope and roll away.

Remix

A cool remix is to turn the Axle Stall into a 50-50 grind. Just come up the ramp at a bigger angle and with a bit more speed, so that when you turn into the stall you grind along on your trucks. Adds a bit of spice to the Axle Stall.

Secret

You don't need a lot of speed to do an Axle Stall, just enough to go over the coping.

Common Problem

My board always sticks to the coping.

Before Step 3, push the tail forward with your back foot so the back trucks slide along until the wheel is touching the coping. This stops the board getting caught up or sticking.

TAIL STALL

A clean-looking move is the best way to describe this trick. Done properly by a top skater it looks just like the board is a part of them. But that is why they are top skaters.

Foot Position

Front foot over the front bolts, back foot on the middle of the tail of the board.

Step 1

You need to roll-up Fakey (backward) and your approach should be straight on.

Step 2

Just as the board reaches the coping push down on the tail to jam it over the coping.

Phil's Tip «

You only need enough speed to make it to the coping.

Common Problem

I always seem to get the wheels over the coping and never Tail Stall.

You are going too fast and you're overshooting. You only need enough speed to be able to touch the coping.

Step 3

Now you are in position, so Drop-In and roll away smiling.

Remix

Do everything the other way around and do a Nose Stall. When he first started, Phil used to spend hours on a half pipe going from Tail Stall to Nose Stall, but it is that practice that has made him so good.

Secret

Gradually build up to a full Tail Stall, but to start with be happy with the tail just touching the coping.

BLUNT FAKEY

Phil can remember how much effort he put into learning the Blunt Fakey, because until he got the movement locked it was quite scary to do.

Foot Position

Front foot lower than the front bolt, back foot on the middle of the tail of the board.

Step 1

Approach straight on and push down at the top of the ramp with your back foot to lift the front wheels up and over the coping.

Step 2

Stall the back wheels over the coping.

Common Problem

I always hang the front wheels up.

Two things: maybe your Ollie isn't hard enough in Step 3, or you're not waiting for the board long enough and trying to land it before the front wheels have gone past the coping.

Step 3

Push down hard on the tail with your back foot to Ollie the board out of the stall. Wait for the board to clear the coping then land it and roll away Fakey.

Remix

This makes something wonderful into something unbelievable: do a 180 to come out of the Blunt in Step 3. This is what Skateboarding is about — taking a great trick and making it even better.

Secret

To get the feel for how hard you need to Ollie in Step 3, just keep your front foot on the board instead of landing it. This way you get the motion right before you try to land it.

Phil's Tip «

To help you when learning the trick, In Step 3 grab the nose of the board and lift it up.

BACKSIDE NOSE BLUNT

This is a hard trick and Phil spent a lot of time getting it locked. He still finds that if he doesn't do it regularly he has to practice just to get back to where he was.

Foot Position

Front foot pointing slightly forward just under the front bolts, with the sole of your back foot on the far rim of the tail.

Step 1

As you approach the coping, twist your upper body across in front of you and use your back foot to scoop the tail around.

Step 2

Lock the nose of the board over the coping with you facing down the slope.

Common Problem

I never lock in the nose and instead Nose Manual away from the coping.

You are going too fast, getting too much air and going past the coping. Still looks good, but not what you want to do.

Step 3

Push down hard with your front foot to Nollie out of the stall, then land it and roll away.

Remix

A terrific way to make a Backside Nose Blunt even better is to really rocket an Ollie into it. Get lots of height, and then drop into it. Just looks unbelievable.

Secret

You don't have much time to do Steps 1 and 2, so begin to twist as soon as you can.

Phil's Tip «

Just practice Step 3 on its own before trying the whole trick.